Affirmations for Black Men

Inspiring and Motivating Words for a Black Man. A Foolproof Shortcut to Success and Significance in Life.

TERREL HUNT

D1522345

Want to Get 234 Life-Changing Affirmations For Free?

Scan This QR code with your smartphone or tablet and Get It NOW!

TABLE OF CONTENT

INTRODUCTION...5

CHAPTER 1: How to Change your Life with the Power of Affirmations 7

CHAPTER 2: Neuroplasticity: The Science and Benefits of Positive Affirmations 14

How Affirmations Reconfigure your Brain........................18

CHAPTER 3: Active or Passive: How to Create Powerful Affirmations that Really Work 23

Making Affirmations Work for You 29

CHAPTER 4: 150 Positive Affirmations for Black Men 31

CHAPTER 5: Tips for Building Confidence and Self-Esteem 39

CONCLUSION 41

"You must learn a new way to think before you can master a new way to be." -- Marianne Williamson

***

"If You Enjoyed This Book, Please Consider Supporting Black Community by Leaving a Review on Amazon. Thank you!"

INTRODUCTION

Black men start life feeling confident, fearless, and unstoppable. They feel like they can take the world on. Then, suddenly, they are hit by the reality of the harsh world they live in. So, their positive attitude becomes lost, and their confidence in the world becomes a thing of the fast.

As a result, they become victims of insecurity and self-defeating behaviors – which can stop them from becoming the best version of themselves. Being a black man means you can probably relate to everything said so far.

Well, the world may not cheer you on; the good thing is that you can be your own cheerleader through the use of positive self-affirmations. Affirmations are powerful. You can change your mindset by practicing them repeatedly. They are a tool for strengthening the connection between your subconscious and conscious mind.

With the use of affirmations, you can inspire and motivate yourself for success in a world that is rigged against you. More importantly, you can boost your self-esteem and self-confidence and work on turning your bright ideas into reality.

This book contains 150+ powerful affirmations that can support you on the path to becoming a powerful, confident, and successful black man. It was written specifically for you so you can change your life.

It's time to harness your inner power and build the life you want!

CHAPTER 1:
How to Change your Life with the Power of Affirmations

I'd like to say that being a black man is all sunshine and rainbows, but you know that it isn't. One of the hardest realizations many black men face on the path to healing is the thought and feeling that we're the odd sheep of society. At least, that is what it seems like to most people – especially if you're a black man in a country such as the United States.

Maybe you've always had that nagging sense of feeling like the proverbial stepsister (stepbrother, in this case). Or you feel like a lone wolf. Or maybe the scapegoat. Of course, this could be due to any reason.

Perhaps it's because you respond to things differently than people of other races who live in the same country as you. Or maybe it's because you look different. It could also be because you made life choices that go against what your community considers "normal."

Anyway, the point is that many black men can relate to that feeling of being the odd one out. However, and for whatever reasons you may have realized this for yourself, I believe that black men can collectively identify with that "black sheep" archetype.

But the goal of this book isn't to help you dwell on this but to give you tips on how you can reclaim the power of this archetype through the use of affirmations.

As a black man, have you ever wondered, "Am I good enough?" If yes, know that millions of black men are with you in this. It can be pretty tough to deal with feelings of inadequacy, inferiority, and worthlessness. These feelings are painful, and they cut to the bone.

Whether they involve never-ending challenges caused by a traumatic past or health challenges or they are evoked by periodic circumstances, many people experience these feelings. But we aren't here to talk about people – we are here to talk specifically about black men.

Aside from the fact that these negative feelings can lead to uncomfortable thoughts and beliefs in the form of "I am not good enough," feelings of inadequacy and inferiority can also negatively impact motivation, performance, competence, and your ability to connect with yourself. And the truth is that the average black man struggles with these feelings far more than we'd like to admit.

Often, I hear people share their experiences about not feeling good enough. This normally has to do with their work, their role in their family, education, ability to form meaningful connections with others, and reaching their career and life goals. Sometimes, it's a direct result of having experienced trauma, suppression, and oppression.

The beautiful aspect of affirmations is that they can help you overcome these feelings and recognize your own self-worth.

The feeling of "I am not good enough" feels like looking into a clouded mirror and not seeing a clear image of who you are. But affirmations can help you take the cloud off this mirror. This is something that is proven by psychologists.

Studies suggest that self-affirmations can help you reduce feelings of powerlessness, see past adversities, increase self-competence, reconnect with your core values, enhance your self-image, and foster healthier thoughts and emotions. All of these, as you may know, is crucial to success in life.

Additionally, self-affirmations improve motivation, focus, performance, health, relationships, and many more outcomes that I'll explain. They are a powerful way for you to connect with yourself, who you truly are, and the things that you are honestly passionate about. In turn, this allows you to connect meaningfully and effectively to the world around you.

At this point, you're probably wondering, "Why should I use affirmations?" I completely understand this question. After all, the concept of affirmations does sound like something people use for laughs on the internet.

However, the fact is that people use self-affirmations for different reasons. Generally speaking, self-affirmations are used to reprogram the mind in order to instill certain beliefs about ourselves, the world, and our role in it.

Self-affirmations can also help you create the reality you wish for – often relating to your career, studies, health, relationship, finances, and overall status in life.

As Dr. Walter E. Jacobson says, affirmations of this nature have a certain value because the subconscious mind plays a key role in the manifestation of our innate desires and our lives as a whole. Put simply, what you believe about yourself subconsciously, can significantly impact the outcome of events in your life.

At the most basic level, when you have a positive attitude about yourself and the world, your life is likely to run as smoothly as possible. Individuals who believe in the "law of attraction" refer to this as raising one's vibration such that when it's positive, we attract all kinds of positive things from love to renewed health and financial abundance.

In contrast, when you have a negative attitude or feel bad about yourself, you subconsciously behave in self-defeating ways, which may lead to problems such as financial instability, acute or chronic illness, or interpersonal drama.

On a pragmatic level, though, it is actually p5`ossible that self-affirmations can reduce symptoms of stress, anxiety, and depression. They can even improve problem-solving performance in chronically stressed people. This means that affirmations may just be the solution if you're underperforming in any area of your life.

At this point, I should define what affirmations are to help you further understand exactly what I'm talking about.

An affirmation is a simple statement designed to motivate self-change in humans. It is something you say to yourself to initiate a shift in mindset and feel better about yourself. It serves as a reminder of what you are, what you want to be, and what you could be.

You can use affirmations as the way to remind yourself about your goals, dreams, and aspirations and help you focus on these things. In itself, this is capable of promoting positive and sustained self-change.

Self-affirmations first became popular in the early 1900s, and since then, they have become instrumental in positive psychology. Many self-help coaches and gurus use them to help clients worldwide. The million-dollar question is, "Do affirmations work?"

Well, according to recent evidence, affirmations do indeed work. In fact, a recently published study by Carnegie Mellon indicates that self-affirmations are capable of protecting the brain against the damaging effect of stress. The evidence also reveals that they can help counteract ego depletion.

Self-affirmations can enhance your performance in assigned tasks and make you more receptive to personal mistakes. Also, they have been proven to help rewrite self-fulfilling prophecies relating to social rejection. In short, affirmations are exactly what you need.

Like many black men, you probably struggle to believe in yourself. Perhaps you also find it hard to have positive thoughts. Or maybe you just can't help creating the worst-case scenarios in your mind. No matter what, affirmations can help you shift your mindset positively in ways that can redefine your life for the best.

I used to believe that the concept of self-affirmations was a new-age trend that amounted to wishful thinking. But after going out of my comfort zone to understand cognitive processes and how powerful internal dialogue can be, I realized that it could potentially determine or influence the course of one's life.

What we say to ourselves matters because it forms the basis of our behavior and action, which, in turn, make up our life experiences. Our inner dialogue also serves as the foundation for our emotional experiences.

This means that when you say bad things to yourself, you create emotions that make you feel bad, and vice versa. You're the only person in charge of your inner dialogue.

Studies have shown that positive self-affirmations can positively affect a range of human behaviors and responses, as previously highlighted. You can positively affirm yourself towards healthy eating, exercise, and other positive health-related behaviors.

Freudian theories have been a major part of psychology for more than a century. Freud explained that the conscious mind was just the tip of the iceberg, with the subconscious mind allowing humans to discuss affirmations and how they impact behavior by using the subconscious mind to influence conscious behavior.

Let's look at it this way for a minute. Humans are repeatedly exposed to advertisements on TV, radio, billboards, social media, etc. These ads all contain key messages that we can consider a subconscious imbibing of affirmations. If the key message in an ad is accepted by the subconscious mind, it inadvertently influences a consumer's decision towards the product or service in the advertisement.

According to the self-affirmation theory, humans are inherently motivated to maintain our global perception and self-integrity. Based on this, it was suggested by the proponents of this theory that awareness of the benefits of self-affirmation could undermine the impact of the affirmations on the participants.

In other words, if you're told to self-affirm in order to reap certain benefits, that challenges your sense of autonomy, which undermines the intrinsic appeal of the affirmations. On the contrary, if you try self-affirmations with the belief that you're doing it of your own free will, then the benefits are restored.

These findings were made in studies about the self-affirmation theory. In two of the studies, some participants were informed of the benefits of affirmations for academic performance and were then either given a choice to do the affirmations or instructed to do them.

In both studies, participants who were informed of the benefits and then instructed to use self-affirmations anyway couldn't get the benefits. However, these benefits were restored when they were given a choice to self-affirm or not.

These examples show that self-affirmation is a choice you must make for yourself if you truly want the benefits. It is suggested that self-affirmations remind us of vital aspects of the self, allowing us to review events from a rational point of view.

By amplifying the psychological resource of global perception and self-integrity, self-affirmation reduces your defensiveness towards seemingly threatening events and information, which can lead to improvement in several aspects of your life.

However, the subconscious mind still can't differentiate between positive and negative or real and imagined. For example, if you want to be confident, you cannot say things like, "I don't want to be a coward."

The mind will focus on the word "coward" and neglect the "don't," which neutralizes the desired result. You have to be careful when choosing things to share with your subconscious mind, and that is why positive self-affirmations are crucial. Sometimes, we feed our minds with negative beliefs without even realizing it.

I have observed that many people find positive affirmations

ineffective or difficult because they try to make positive statements about things they don't truly believe in. This is due to the brain's tendency to resist huge leaps in thinking.

If you say "I'm brave" to yourself while feeling completely terrified and anxious internally, then you're lying to yourself, and your brain knows it. This can cause your brain to trigger something I refer to as "resistant thinking," which only worsens your situation.

An example of a resistant thought along this line could be – *This is silly. I am silly. Why am I saying something that would never work for myself? etc.*

Another downside to saying affirmations that you don't really believe in or care to believe in is the possibility of pushing your mind to dig for evidence that contradicts your new affirmation. An example of that would be – *Of course, this is silly. I know I'm not brave; everyone knows it. The thought of speaking my mind to my boss makes me feel faint, like that last meeting where I shitted the bed and wished the ground could open up and swallow me.*

Self-affirmations only work if they are realistic and within the realm of what you consider the truth. Still, it can be pretty challenging to find thoughts and beliefs that aren't too much of a leap from your current state of mind.

The brain is an intriguing organ. Most of the time, all it wants to do is jump straight to the finish line. Thus, if you're fighting insecurity and trying to come up with a positive self-statement to improve your insecurities, you're likely to go straight to "I'm confident."

Now, that may be all good, but the question is, are you really confident? Do you even believe that you're truly confident? In a subsequent chapter, I will give pointers on how you can come up with affirmations that accurately portray your reality and current state of mind.

But before then, let's delve into the science behind affirmations and why many people believe in their power.

CHAPTER 2:
Neuroplasticity: The Science and Benefits of Positive Affirmations

Every second of every day, your body experiences physical changes in response to the thoughts in your head. When you think about something, your brain immediately sends signals and releases neurotransmitters that trigger one or more physical changes in your body.

Neurotransmitters are the chemicals that control your mood, feelings, and all bodily functions. Over time, through neuroplasticity, it's been established that our thoughts affect our cells, genes, and brain. In other words, they change our bodies.

For example, when you express gratitude for something, your body triggers a surge of dopamine, norepinephrine, and other rewarding neurotransmitters. This, in turn, causes a general uplifting of your mind.

This shows that the things you think and believe about yourself can impact your body, mind, and life. Affirmations can help you harness this power. As we've established, they help you respond to challenges and adversities in a less combative and resistant way. Affirmations are a way for you to improve your sense of self and make your brain more resilient.

As humans, we have an ongoing dialogue in our heads throughout our day. Some of this dialogue can be beneficial for our mind and body, while some hold us back. The ones that hold us back are "fear statements" that are counterproductive to our growth and wellbeing.

Listening to yourself worry about not being enough, never being successful, what you've missed out on in life, or replaying anxious moments is unhelpful. Affirmations can help you counter and subsequently quiet these fear statements and negative thoughts in your head.

They can help challenge these self-defeating thoughts. Just as repetitive physical exercise can make your body stronger, self-affirmations can strengthen your mind – making it less susceptible to negative thoughts and beliefs.

Training yourself to think differently is crucial to getting rid of the pain pathways in your brain and replacing them with new ones. This is what it means to reprogram your brain and prep it for success. Of course, affirmations are your key to achieving this.

As I previously said, they can help you break bad habits and form new, healthy ones. In a neurologic sense, pain is a habit that you need to break if you want to mature into a better version of yourself.

The science of affirmations is founded upon psychological theories and clinical studies. In the previous chapter, I talked briefly about the self-affirmation theory, which is one of the leading theories that is used to explain the "why" and "how" of positive affirmations.

Empirical studies suggest that humans maintain our sense of self-identity by affirming our beliefs in positive ways. According to Cohen and Sherman (2014), self-efficacy is how we protect ourselves from potential threats by using affirmations to increase our resilience.

Self-affirmations have been used effectively to increase physical activity in humans. In fact, they helped people in a study (Epton and Harris, 2008) eat more fruits and vegetables.

Affirmations can help you cultivate a more optimistic outlook on yourself and your experiences. Optimism is one of the most powerful concepts in positive psychology. Sometimes, chronic pain is caused by a destructive narrative in our heads. But you can change this narrative through affirmations and journaling.

Neuroplasticity, also known as brain plasticity, refers to the brain's ability to adapt due to experience. When I say that the brain possesses plasticity, it doesn't mean that the human brain is plastic or similar to plastic.

Neuro stands for *neurons*, the nerve cells that make up the brain and the nervous system. Plasticity, on the other hand, means that the brain is malleable – i.e., capable of change. The brain consists of 86 billion neurons – approximately.

It is believed that neurogenesis – the formation of new neurons – stops shortly after birth. Today, researchers have shown that the brain is capable of forming new pathways, reorganizing old ones, and even generating new neurons. And that is what neuroplasticity is.

I'm not getting into the deeply scientific aspect of neuroplasticity, but you should know that there are two types of brain plasticity. The first is functional plasticity, which is when the brain moves its functions from a damaged area to an undamaged area of the brain. The second is structural plasticity, which is when the brain rebuilds its physical structure based on learning.

Brain plasticity has so many benefits. Its primary function is to help the brain and change, which, in turn:

- improves the brain's ability to learn new things
- enhances existing cognitive abilities
- helps recover from trauma and brain injuries
- strengthens lost or declining brain functions
- promotes brain fitness

Now, one important question is, "How does brain plasticity work?" The answer to this question is your key to understanding how affirmations are capable of making such significant changes to the brain and a person as a whole.

At birth, the cerebral cortex's neurons compose of approximately 2,500 synapses each. By the time an infant reaches age three, this number has increased to an astounding 15,000 synapses in each neuron. The point here is that the first few years of infancy are meant for rapid brain growth.

However, the average adult brain is only composed of half that number of synapses. This is because the brain strengthens some connections and eliminates others as we grow older and gain new experiences. This is called synaptic pruning.

Basically, the neurons that we use frequently become stronger, while the ones we rarely use die off. Through synaptic pruning, the brain adapts itself to the changing environment caused by our growth.

There are a few defining characteristics of brain plasticity.

- **Age and environment:** Although neuroplasticity occurs throughout a person's lifetime, some changes happen predominantly at certain ages. The brain experiences major changes in the early phase of development, especially as it grows and reorganizes. Generally, younger brains are more receptive to experiences than older ones. This means that it's best to start affirmations as early as possible in life. Of course, this isn't to say that adult brains are incapable of affirmations-induced adaptation.

- **Ongoing:** Brain plasticity never ends. It is an ongoing process that continues through an individual's lifetime. It is continually induced through experience, learning, memory formation, and in some cases, brain damage. So, contrary to the belief that the brain remains static after a specific age, it never stops adapting in response to learning and experience. This means that you can keep using affirmations for as long as you live. They can be your go-to whenever you want to make little or significant changes in your life.

- **Limitations:** There are certain limits to the brain's malleability. It's not infinitely adaptive. Some parts of the brain are responsible for major functions and actions. Damage to the brain can affect the functions of these areas. Although recovery may happen, other parts of the brain cannot take over the functions of the affected areas.

As I said, there are different ways to encourage brain plasticity. Some of them include enriching your learning opportunities. For example, you could try learning a new language, a musical instrument, or a new skill.

However, we'll be focusing on how you can use positive self-affirmations to encourage your brain to change and adapt according to your environment.

How Affirmations Reconfigure your Brain

There's a phrase that goes, "Neurons that wire together fire together." The meaning of this phrase is quite straightforward, but many do not get it. When a nerve cell (neuron) wants to communicate with another, it does this through an electrochemical signal.

This electrochemical signal is released from the cell body and travels through the axon until it reaches the synaptic left, i.e., the space between two nerve cells. Since the signal can't cross this space, it converts into a neurotransmitter, which is capable of diffusing across the synapse.

From there, the neurotransmitter attaches to a receptor cell on the opposite side. Its molecule binds with the receptor, causing the release of an electrical charge which is transported to the second neuron via the dendrite.

This link between the nerve cells is called an electrochemical pathway. Many of these neurotransmitters have unique emotional signatures. For example, oxytocin creates feelings of attachment and trust, while adrenocorticotropic hormone (ACTH) triggers the release of cortisol, creating feelings of arousal. As Candace Pert said, neurotransmitters are "molecules of emotion."

Neurotransmitters are essentially chemicals that affect how you feel due to their interaction with your emotional brain (limbic system) and the autonomic nervous system, as well as the immune, digestive, and respiratory systems.

To simply everything I've been saying so far, this means that a neurochemical response is triggered when you think a specific thought, remember something or say something aloud in your head. Then, the feelings associated with that neurochemical response ripple through your body.

For example, when you feel stressed because of certain thoughts, it is because those thoughts activate your sympathetic nervous system, triggering feelings of arousal. Depending on the intensity of the feeling, you may also experience physiological responses in the form of a dry mouth, clammy pals, etc.

Every human being repeats certain thought patterns that have negative consequences because of how they make us feel about ourselves. These thoughts have become habitual, and they impair our ability to dream, pursue our goals and reach a state of genuine happiness and fulfillment.

In fact, these thoughts can adversely affect our immune system and increase our white T cell count. You may already know this, but an increased white T cell count means inflammation, which is when the body thinks it is being attacked.

Just as negative thoughts can adversely affect us, positive thought patterns induce positive responses in the brain. That can lead to increased confidence, happiness, and overall wellbeing. Thus, it comes as no surprise that happier people generally enjoy a positive mindset. They also cultivate positive thinking, which improves their health and allows them to deal with stress better.

Let's look at it this way. You have probably sat for an exam before, and you probably know that your state of mind during an exam isn't just important; it is the key to success in an examination. If you enter an exam feeling upbeat and confident, you're more likely to perform to expectations.

The point here is that certain thoughts elicit associated feelings, which, in turn, affect your overall disposition and your tendency towards certain behaviors (good or bad). Your thoughts help you create your stance within and toward the world. Consequentially, your experiences influence your thoughts, and that helps to change your worldview.

As you can see, this makes the concept of self-affirmations seem less age-y and trendy than it does to people who don't understand it. The fact is that everyone wants happiness, abundance, success, and satisfaction in life.

If changing the way you think and view the world can help you achieve that, you should know that you can attain that over time.

As previously noted, we all have some patterns of thinking and behaving that have become habitual. Sometimes, we attempt to change these habits, only to find that we're falling into the same old patterns – even though it doesn't make us feel good.

Considering that different parts of the brain are naturally connected through the wiring of neurons, these habitual thinking and behaving patterns become hardwired. When you add this to the fact that it's easy to become addicted to the neurotransmitters released when our neurons fire, you can see how much of a tricky situation this is.

Every time you subconsciously give in to a specific stimulus, you activate some neural pathways and the areas of the brain housing their neurons. As you habitually activate these areas, they become denser.

This could be because the associated neurons in these areas branch out and form connections with other neurons. It could also be because the neurons increase blood flow or the number of cells in these areas.

The more you respond to a stimulus that activates these areas in your daily life, the more you indulge in the related habits.

Let's look at an example to help further you understand how this works. The release of dopamine activates the neural connections that push us towards behaviors that can help us accomplish our goals.

You feel good when that dopamine hits because it plays a role in the reward pathways. This can be pretty helpful when you're trying to swap out negative thoughts and beliefs for positive ones. For example, suppose you catch yourself negatively judging yourself based on something someone else said. In that case, you can replace that negative judgmental thought with a positive one.

When you successfully do this, you're most likely to get a hit of dopamine that is triggered by the feeling of stopping that destructive thought or belief from affecting you negatively. In that case, you get a reward because you followed through on the decision to replace negative thoughts with positive ones.

The ability to do this – recognize negative thought patterns and replace them with negative ones – is what distinguishes human psychology and logicality. An executive mental function like this occurs in the cerebral cortex – which is the part of the brain in charge of goal setting and long-term planning.

Neurons respond to experiences that could be in the form of thoughts, stimuli, etc. Every time the neural pathway is activated, the neural connection between nerve cells in various parts of the brain grows stronger and denser.

The stronger this connection, the harder it is to break thought and behavioral patterns. Not surprisingly, our behavioral tendencies influence how we experience the world, as well as how the perception of ourselves.

This means that we start to identify with certain ways of thinking and behaving, and erroneously believe that it is who we truly are.

Fortunately, affirmations can help us shortcut neural connections, rewire our brains, and as a consequence, change our self-perception.

By changing these patterns and adopting new thoughts and beliefs, you can take advantage of your brain's malleability to recreate yourself.

One thing you must know is that affirmations do not work in isolation. You must use them as part of an overall reprogramming and healing process.

Affirmations won't "fix" your pain. The point of practicing affirmations is to help your brain create new pathways and circuits in response to them. But you must also let yourself experience the physical or mental pain you're feeling before redirecting it.

Please, don't confuse positive affirmations with positive thinking, as these are two different things. Positive thinking helps to suppress negativity. I'm not asking you to allow yourself to enjoy the pain you're in; it's impossible to win that battle. It's much different to maintain a positive outlook on life and your experiences consistently.

The point is that there is sufficient research showing that self-affirmations can be used to treat different conditions, especially psychological ones. Based on available evidence, you can use it for chronic pain, migraines, and neuroplastic conditions.

Fortunately, it's quite easy to incorporate positive affirmations into one's life. You can do it via meditation or journaling, and all it'd take to start reaping the benefits is a few minutes of daily practice. The more you practice, the more your brain adapts.

Before you know it, you'd have adapted to affirmations and mastered the art of using them for different issues and goals in your life.

CHAPTER 3:
Active or Passive: How to Create Powerful Affirmations that Really Work

There are different approaches to creating affirmations that really work, but not all are effective. Yes, this book contains affirmations that you can recite daily to improve your life. However, there is nothing more powerful than affirmations you create by yourself.

For affirmations to work as you want them to, they must internalize things that you truly believe. If you don't believe in the statement you're affirming to yourself, your brain won't believe or accept it too.

Now, affirmations can be active or passive; it depends on how you approach the practice. Essentially, active affirmations are the positive statements you recite out loud to yourself for a daily boost of confidence. They could also be statements you write down in your journal.

Passive affirmations, on the other hand, refer to affirmations recited by someone else for you to listen to. Of course, they could also be recited by you for yourself. The difference here is that you recite active affirmations while you listen to passive ones in the form of audio recordings.

Your subconscious mind is most open to affirmations when in the "alpha" brainwave state, which is when the mind is most relaxed. Repeatedly using positive self-affirmations in a meditative state can help you manifest positive changes in different areas of your life.

The alpha wave frequency is achieved during a meditative state or right before one falls asleep, which is the optimal time for your mind to receive positive affirmations. There is music designed specifically to induce the alpha wave state for those who aren't prone to reaching that state. Audio affirmations tend to come with music that can help you reach that meditative state.

One of the best times to listen to passive affirmations is right before you sleep or even during sleep. The unconscious mind does not go to sleep when you do. In fact, that is the time when it is most alert because the conscious mind would have retired already.

When you listen to recorded affirmations right before or during sleep, your subconscious or unconscious mind receives and absorbs every information from the recording. That means you can take advantage of both types of affirmations.

In other words, you can compose powerful affirmative statements yourself, record them in your own voice, and listen to them every night before and during sleep, which is when your mind is most likely to be in the calmest state to accept everything you say in your affirmations.

To create affirmations that actually do what they are meant to do, there are a few things to keep in mind. First, you must observe your current behavioral patterns and identify the ones that are against your best interests. It's also important to recognize which aspects of your health and wellbeing you struggle the most with. Using that knowledge, you can make affirmations that are likely to trigger the biggest changes for you.

Second, you must be motivated enough to take action. Once you accept that your subconscious doesn't always align with what you want for yourself, you can take steps to solve the problems through the repetitive use of affirmations.

However, it's not enough to repeat random positive affirmations; you can't initiate significant change that way. If you want effective and successful affirmations, you must construct them in the right ways.

That way, you're likely to achieve more positive thoughts, feelings, actions, and experiences with the use of positive affirmations. So, here are some tips to keep in mind when creating your list of positive affirmations.

1. Speak and repeat them aloud

Speaking reinforces learning and makes your subconscious more susceptible to your request. In other words, your subconscious mind is more likely to accept a statement if you speak it out loud instead of just thinking it in your head.

It also helps to add other senses of perceptions; that increases your mind's susceptibility to whatever you tell it. For example, lighting an incense stick every time you practice your affirmations can help your subconscious narrow its focus on the things you say.

Another way to awaken your senses is to ring a bell or something similar before you start repeating your affirmations. The goal here is to create a sort of ritual for your mind to associate with the affirmations.

By doing this, your subconscious mind recognizes that you're demanding its attention every time you repeat the associated ritual.

2. Use present tenses

Your subconscious mind lives in the now, which is why its thinking is simplistic. The mind finds it hard to comprehend concepts like "later" or 'soon." It certainly doesn't find abstract adjectives like "better" easier to understand.

Therefore, it's crucial that you keep your affirmations simple and "at the moment." The best and only way to do this is to use present tenses when constructing positive statements. For example, it's better to say "I am healthy and wealthy" than to say "I am becoming healthier and wealthier with age."

The former statement is much simpler and more straightforward for the subconscious mind to understand. And that is why you're more likely to wow your conscious mind with lofty statements and ideas.

Believe me; the subconscious isn't as easily seduced by statements not rooted in the present.

3. Avoid negatives

It's easy for the subconscious mind to confuse negatives and their true meanings. For example, if you say, "I am not cowardly anymore," your subconscious may highlight the idea of being cowardly since that is the subject of your affirmation.

The same goes for any other affirmative statement with "not." So, be careful to choose words that convey exactly what you mean to your subconscious. That is the only way you can communicate effectively with your mind and trigger the positive change that will lead to the elimination of negative thought patterns.

4. Be specific and direct

Your subconscious can help you achieve the things you want, but it can't do that without some form of guidance and direction from you. Affirmations aren't meant to be vague or generic; they must be as specific as possible.

This doesn't mean that you have to be explicit or go into details as much as possible. For example, a simple statement like "I am strong and healthy" will suffice. Let's say you're looking for a well-paying job. In that case, you have to be specific. After all, "well-paying" is subjective, depending on your goals and expectations.

A simple and direct affirmation for a well-paying job could go like this, "I make $200 000 per annum working for a creative company in California. I am making people happy and having fun with my work. I am respected by my coworkers. I have plenty of time to spend with loved ones."

This is a long affirmation, but it is simple, specific, and direct, just as positive affirmations should be. Once you compose a positive statement that you believe is good for you, practice it out loud and see how you feel.

If you don't feel good when you say it aloud, rework the statement until it becomes an affirmation that makes you feel better about yourself.

5. Focus on solving problems

Successful affirmations focus on solutions, not problems. Saying something like, "I am done with binge eating," can backfire because the focus is on the bad habit instead of the good one you plan to replace it with.

Create affirmations that highlight the positive outcome you desire. "I am succeeding in my work and achieving everything I want to" is an excellent example of an affirmation that focuses on the positive outcome.

The goal of a positive affirmation is to highlight your wants and desires as genuine and authentic without focusing on how dissatisfied you are with your present circumstances. Focus on the changes and improvements you desire, not the bad things you wish to change.

6. Be passionate

Passion infuses affirmations with more power. Self-affirmations are more likely to create the impact you want if they are full of emotion. You have to feel the change or improvement you desire; that is how to make your self-affirmations work.

When you say "I am happy," you should search within yourself and find that feeling. Then, draw into it and let it feel your heart with joy. Do this before you say your positive affirmation out loud.

You will find that the words are so much stronger when they are imbued with the feelings you want to experience. If you imbue your affirmations with positive feelings, they become much more powerful. That makes them more likely to bring about the change or improvement you desire.

Positive affirmations are central to successful self-affirmations.

7. Visualize

The conscious mind can be quite helpful in your journey to reprogram your subconscious mind. You can use it to visualize scenes that reinforce your affirmations. As you know, one picture speaks a thousand words.

Visualization can help you get the exact message you're conveying about your needs and wants across to your subconscious mind. If you're job-hunting, visualize the ideal job in your mind, and add as many details as possible, so your mind knows exactly what you want.

The clearer you can picture the things you desire in your mind, the higher the chance of your subconscious seeing and understanding it.

8. Ground yourself

Grounding your affirmations in your body makes them more likely to affect the changes you want. When practicing the positive statements, add facial expressions, gestures, and sounds that support the affirmations. That can help your body really accept the message.

Another way to achieve this is to practice your affirmations during a brisk walk. Repeat your affirmations over and over as you walk to a chosen destination. Doing this reinforces the mental-somatic pathways in your brain, which further supports your affirmations.

9. Be consistent

Consistency is key to successful affirmations. Choose a time of the day to repeat these positive statements for at least 10 minutes daily and stick to it. Reprogramming your brain takes time. Set reminders, so you don't miss a practice.

You can put up sticky notes around your home paint a twig, rock, or pinecone as a trigger. Every time you see or think about the painted object, state your affirmations out loud. A good alternative is to add reminders to your calendar or even write yourself a letter.

Persistency is important if you want to redefine what goes on in your subconscious, so keep at it. Before you know it, you'll start noticing the desired changes.

10. Take action

It's simply not enough to say things; you must take actions to match. Affirmations aren't magical, and as I said, they don't work in isolation. To ground your affirmations in reality, you have to take action.

If you want a specific job, send out resumes to job descriptions that match what you want. If you want to cultivate healthy eating, get rid of the junk foods in your fridge and buy healthier produce.

If you want to be fitter, repeat your affirmations as you work out in the gym or jog around your neighborhood. Actions always speak louder than words, and taking action tells your subconscious brain you really want the thing (s) you're asking for.

Making Affirmations Work for You

Deliberate thought patterns can become automatic over time if you know how to make them work for you. Yes, the more you repeat affirmations, the easier it is for the thoughts to imprint on your mind.

However, making affirmations work for you requires more than just repeating them every chance you get. As previously noted, consistency or repetition won't matter if you don't believe in the things you're saying.

There are different kinds of positive affirmations. Black men may have qualities that enjoin us, but every black man is still different from the next. Therefore, it is best to use affirmations that connect with how you feel about yourself or the world.

For example, if you prefer to say "I am good enough," another black man might prefer "I am strong and healthy." It all depends on the person.

Nonetheless, you can explore the following affirmations to find some that make you feel better about yourself. Of course, the next chapter contains 200 affirmations that you can choose from at will. But these are just examples to help you recognize and understand which affirmations work for you.

- I am strong.
- I am courageous.
- I am a black man of value.
- I am good enough.
- I am capable of change.
- I am worthy of love.
- I deserve everything I have.
- I have the power to dream and accomplish.
- I grow every day.
- I am grateful for the opportunities that I have.
- I have potentials
- My life is ahead of me

If you believe affirmations can help you, then journaling will support that belief. You can make affirmations work for you through daily journaling. Consider writing a few affirmations in your journal every morning or exploring other journaling ideas to motivate yourself.

It also helps to elaborate on the affirmations you write; that can help strengthen them. For instance, if the affirmation is "I am full of love," you might write down the exact loving feelings or thoughts you have.

Starting a daily affirmation practice is a sure way to cultivate more positive thoughts and emotions and ensure your brain accepts all that positivity. Don't expect magic, though. Your improvements will be small, and they will happen gradually.

But over time, they'll cumulate to a significant change in your life and improve how you feel about yourself.

CHAPTER 4:
150 Positive Affirmations for Black Men

As a black man, you're regularly subjected to adversities and negativities that could make life seem harder than it has to be. However, wouldn't it be nice if you could supercharge your life and make it through these difficulties?

Well, you can with the help of the affirmations below. These affirmations are meant to help every black man to keep pressing on. They also serve as a reminder that you are capable of making positive changes in your life. Most importantly, they remind you that, no matter what, you deserve good things in life.

If you're ready to change your thinking and forge a better path for yourself in life, these 200 affirmations curated specifically for black men will help you. You can read one per day or choose a few to use in your mornings and evenings.

Don't forget that the more you read, the more your brain will start believing them. Before you know it, you'd find yourself on the shortcut to success as a black man. Please note that these affirmations cover all aspects of life from career to finances, health and wellbeing, education, and relationships – both personal and professional.

1. I am deserving of everything good.
2. My color makes me unique.
3. I am proud of who I am.
4. I believe in my cultural heritage.
5. I will never lower my standards because of my color.
6. I am loving and beautiful.

7. I am confident in my truth.

8. I am black, proud, and male.

9. I am blessed with everything I own.

10. I am rising slowly but steadily.

11. I refuse to feel less about myself.

12. I am worthy of a love like every human.

13. I can forge my own path.

14. I am responsible for my successes.

15. I have a place in the world.

16. I am capable of being anything I want to be.

17. I am a beacon of light and hope to my community.

18. I draw strength in my color.

19. My color and features are magnificent.

20. I am a wonderful creation of nature.

21. I create my own destiny. I create my own luck.

22. I am attuned to my ancestors.

23. I am black and beautiful.

24. I will make it through each day, and my attitude will remain positive.

25. I am a work in progress, and my progress is never-ending. I can do better. I can do more. I will always do more.

26. The actions of others have no significant impact on my thoughts, feelings, or life.

27. I don't have to be perfect. I am good enough.

28. I will face my challenges like a grown-up and overcome them the best way I can.

29. My skin color matters. My voice matters. My beliefs matter. I matter.

30. I am in the world to live, not die. I am here for everything, not nothing.

31. I will make the right choices and achieve my goals.
32. I am proud of the man I am shaping up to be.
33. I am competent in my field, and that makes me confident.
34. I can change the world if I so desire.
35. I am capable of changing my thoughts.
36. I am shaping up to be the best version of myself.
37. My deepest desires will be fulfilled now.
38. I am capable of selling my talent.
39. I can't be controlled by the opinions of others.
40. I am powerful and confident.
41. I am smart and great at my job.
42. I have confidence in my body and looks.
43. I am sexy attractive, and I have a good vibe.
44. I won't fake who I am to impress people.
45. I like who I am.
46. I deserve success.
47. People who don't respect me won't have a place in my life.
48. I am witty and intelligent.
49. I attract positive things to myself.
50. I embrace my blackness and my masculinity.
51. I am in love with the true me.
52. I am a magnet to opportunities.
53. I surround myself with other strong black men.
54. I own my life and destiny.
55. I am disciplined and focused.
56. I am at peace with myself.
57. I am fearless and courageous.
58. I am in charge of my health and career.
59. I can achieve anything I want.

60. I believe in my skills and capabilities.
61. I admire myself, and so do others.
62. I am a fighter, and I am not giving up.
63. I am important to myself, my loved ones, and the world.
64. I will work hard to meet my goals.
65. I am determined to be successful.
66. I can do this again.
67. I am productive.
68. I will have a great day.
69. I will make things work for me.
70. I am going to meet my goals today.
71. I am going to have a positive outlook on life today.
72. I will invest in my personal development today.
73. I am grateful for the things I have.
74. I can make my friends and family happy.
75. I am doing well, and I can do better.
76. Life is beautiful.
77. Being black is beautiful.
78. I can finish my tasks.
79. I am talented enough for my field.
80. I will pursue my dreams until I achieve them.
81. I am an asset in any team I am.
82. I will make the best of my career.
83. I am valuable, and so are my ideas and opinions.
84. I love my career.
85. I can build and maintain healthy relationships at work.
86. I care about health as much as my career.
87. Anybody will be lucky to have me.
88. I inspire the best in everyone in my life.

89. People enjoy being around me.

90. I am a lovable one.

91. I deserve respect and admiration.

92. I will not be taken for granted.

93. I deserve the energy I give out in my relationships.

94. I deserve to be happy.

95. I value the people I have a relationship with.

96. I am trying my best.

97. I learn from failures and take them as opportunities for growth.

98. I feel empowered in my career.

99. I can change how I respond to other people.

100. I become stronger and more resilient every day

101. I choose happiness and joy.

102. I see the positives in my situation.

103. I am the only one who dictates how I feel.

104. My body is fueled by healthy food and exercise.

105. I love my life.

106. I feel peaceful in the present moment.

107. I turn negative thoughts into positive beliefs.

108. I am creative and innovative.

109. Nobody does my job as well as me.

110. I believe in my aspirations.

111. People value my ideas and opinions.

112. I am valuable to my team, my family, my friends, and my community.

113. I am giving and nurturing.

114. I give and receive love.

115. I am thoughtful and loving.

116. I treat my loved ones with compassion.

117.I am enthusiastic and fun to be around them.

118.I can confidently express my needs and feelings.

119.My needs should be met in my relationships.

120.Giving up isn't an option for me.

121.I am connected to my roots.

122.My mind is filled with creative ideas.

123.I am the reason for my own happiness.

124.I can build my future and that of my generation to come.

125.I will grow up but won't give up.

126.I am happy with my life.

127.I am free from negativity.

128.I can achieve any lifestyle I want.

129.I have a strong belief system.

130.I will build a healthier lifestyle for myself.

131.I will flourish in my chosen path.

132.I am aligned with my higher consciousness.

133.I am a blessing to the world.

134.I am an inspiring black man.

135.I was born to be great and impactful.

136.I can change the world with my thoughts and beliefs.

137.I live my life honestly.

138.I possess the great qualities of my ancestors.

139.I recognize my power as a strong man of color.

140.I have my own beauty and magnificence.

141.I am in harmony with nature.

142.I am the best husband and father.

143.I have clear goals in life.

144.I welcome change with open arms.

145.Fear has no power over me.

146. I will reach the greatest heights possible.
147. I choose love over hate.
148. I believe in myself and my community.
149. My patience keeps me going.
150. I am proud of my heritage.

Apart from these affirmations, which you're meant to recite yourself, there are affirmations that you can get other people to read out loud to you. Having others affirm you can be incredibly helpful in your journey. So, find a trusted friend or family member to read the following to you.

• You are loved and respected. The world may rage against you. People may hate you in different spheres of love. But none of that matters because you are loved. Beautiful black man, you are loved by your creator, mother, father, siblings. We love you more deeply than you could ever imagine. And you are capable of giving and receiving love. Your love can bring about peace, healing, joy, and restoration.

• You are worth everything to the world. Your blackness isn't a target; it is your superpower. No matter how hard the world tries to diminish your dignity, remember that your dignity is an inherent gift bestowed upon you by the creator. Beautiful black man, you are valued. You have dignity. You are worth infinitely more than you know. You are special.

• Beautiful black man, the world needs you. Your community needs you. We need you. You are a natural-born leader. We need your strength. We need your business acumen. We need your voice. We wish to receive healing from you. We need the power of your joy. The community needs your pride, your magic, and your leadership.

• You can succeed because you have what it takes. You aren't afraid to think and take action. You aren't afraid to prioritize your health and wellbeing. You deserve to reach the heights you desire. You deserve to take care of yourself.

- Powerful black man, you can change the world with your influence. You will inspire generations. You will rule nations. You will lead armies. You will become everything you desire. Your income will change for the better. You are a game-changer, and you will always rise to the occasion.

- You can push through adversities. Keep pressing on. Life may be hard for you, but you will achieve everything you want. You are destined for more.

- Hope keeps you going even things seem bleak. You have your life ahead of you. You will find peace. You will gain strength in the divine. You will find help in troubled times. You will rise out of despair into eternal hope.

If you aren't comfortable asking someone to read these to you, then consider role-playing in front of your mirror. Read these positive statements out loud to your reflection in the mirror and make sure you feel the power of each word.

I hope that these affirmations serve as a solid guide for you to create your own personal practice. Don't forget that you have to practice daily if you want to acquire the benefits of positive affirmations fully.

Also, don't just stick to these affirmations. They are vague and generic, so they can apply to every black man on earth. Instead, create your own affirmations using this framework. Practice daily, and you will start to see changes in your confidence, resilience, relationships, career, and physical and emotional wellbeing.

CHAPTER 5:
Tips for Building Confidence and Self-Esteem

As you may already know, confidence is the key to becoming a successful black man. So, it's natural to be curious about how you can become more confident by raising your self-esteem. Many black men are in the same boat as you. In fact, most of us struggle with confidence at some point in our lives.

This is especially true when you're just starting out in life or when you are a bit mature. It's not a bad thing to question your confidence because that's a sign of self-perception. Changing your self-talk can help build confidence, and you can achieve that through positive affirmations.

However, that isn't the only step you can take to improve self-confidence and self-esteem. The secret to confidence is in your self-perception, which, in turn, affects your self-esteem. Although many people use self-confidence, self-esteem, and self-perception interchangeably, they are actually different interconnected concepts. That is true in a world where black men are expected to be alpha males.

Self-confidence is defined as a belief in one's personal judgment and decision-making skills. Self-esteem is an evaluation of your sense of self-worth. Self-perception is a set of beliefs you have about yourself.

Evidently, these are three similar but distinct terms. It's important to remember these words and their meanings as you navigate your journey to becoming a more confident black man.

Before you go further, I want you to familiarize yourself with *mindfulness*, which is the awareness of the here and now.

Mindfulness engages the five senses, and people use it for different reasons. For example, bodybuilders use it to gain more muscle mass.

Now that you understand this, here are some tips to help you build your confidence and self-esteem.

- Believe that you are capable of making sound decisions. This is one of the keys to becoming more confident. Affirm to yourself that you're intelligent and experienced enough to make healthy decisions. The remaining tips depend on your ability to do this.
- Learn to tune out negative thoughts and feelings. You can achieve this by grounding yourself at the moment through mindfulness-based meditation. Self-confidence is achievable if you can learn to ignore negative thoughts about the past or the future.
- Accept your mistakes and learn from them. Don't be ashamed or embarrassed; mistakes are a vital part of life. We would be incapable of learning without them. Your mistakes are yours to learn from.
- Highlight your physical, intellectual, and personal strengths and assets when doing a self-review. Think about all the positive things you can say about yourself; those are your assets.
- Be grateful. Gratitude empowers self-affirmations. It can directly and positively impact your self-esteem. Use mindfulness-based meditation to remind yourself of all the good things you should be grateful for.
- Practice self-care. Universally, confident black men take self-care seriously. In short, this means accepting that it's OK to want to improve your personal appearance. Invest in a skincare routine for men to make your melanin pop even more. Do what you need to look like the best and most attractive version of yourself.

Every confident man you'll come across follows the above tips. With confidence, you can attract better jobs, better income, and respect from everyone around you. You can believe in yourself and accept yourself for who you are.

Don't Forget To Pick Your FREE BONUS!

Scan This QR code with your smartphone or tablet and Get It NOW!

CONCLUSION

My hope for you is that these affirmations become more than mere words, that they build the foundation for you to become the man you desire. I hope that they serve as the foundations of your new identity so that when the world tries to label you as anything else, you immediately recognize that it is a lie.

Self-esteem is affected by how you view yourself. Be intentional about changing the ways you view or think about yourself. When you're feeling insecure or doubtful about yourself, remember that affirmations can remind you of who you are.

Ignore the identity the world tries to pin on you and forge your own path. Remember that you are cherished, and you're in life to fulfill a purpose bigger than you. Every single step you take will lead you to your destiny.

Remember that mistakes are normal. So, when you take a misstep, correct yourself with grace and continue on your desired path. The world needs you more than you realize because you matter greatly.

Good luck, powerful and confident black man!

Are you looking to surprise your wife, friend, mom, or daughter?

Would you like to help your loved one uncover the female part of "Powerful Affirmations?"

Here is a book I recommend from my fellow author Deja Tomlinson:

Click the link below and get it now.

Once you click on this link, you'll see all the raving reviews and how other people loved this book.

Made in the USA
Las Vegas, NV
13 April 2023

70522924R00024